Insights 4
The Path

By Dr. Jaya Sonkar, MD MPH

Photograph by: Dr. Jaya Sonkar MD MPH

HOBBIES AND HAPPINESS CREATIONS
Texas, USA

Published by Hobbies and Happiness Creations 2024
Copyright Dr. Jaya Sonkar MD MPH 2025

Dedication

This book is dedicated to my daughter, Ms. Riya Agarwal; my beloved parents, Mr. Ram Baboo Sonkar and Mrs. Ranjana Sonkar; and my cherished family and friends. I extend my heartfelt gratitude to my teachers, patients, colleagues, business partners, vendors, and everyone I have ever met. Each meeting and every interaction has contributed to my learning journey, and the process continues.

Preface

It has been a journey, a long one, and there is still a long way to go.

Just when I feel I have learned a great deal, something happens to remind me that I have only touched the edges of a small pond, while an ocean of lessons still waits to be discovered.

Medicine is one of the noblest professions. It brings us close to countless lives and gives us the privilege of helping others. Along the way, it offers moments of realization, experiences to grow from, and lessons that shape who we are.

Whether it is the happiest, most content patient or one who is deeply distressed, each carries a unique story filled with wisdom.

Exploring and learning may not have been the goal at the beginning, but they become the very essence of the journey. From beginning to end, life is full of possibilities and opportunities, chances to make choices, to learn from them, and to gather pearls of wisdom along the way.

And perhaps the end is not an end at all, but the beginning of a journey beyond boundaries!

A Note to My Readers

Life is short, even if it lasts a hundred years. Along the way, we will experience everything: joy and sorrow, success and failure, love and even betrayal. We should just expect it, let it come, and then let it pass. Watch it all as if we are spectators, and take the lessons life offers. We should neither let excitement nor despair affect us.

Not long ago, a kind and noble teacher who works with children with special needs shared her struggles. She was trying to stay calm in the middle of her challenges.

The truth is simple: We should do what we can. And what we cannot do, we shouldn't punish ourself for it.

We are human. If we were meant to be perfect, we would not be here. We are not gods. We are here to learn, to stumble, and to grow.

As long as our intentions are good and we give it our best effort, there is nothing to regret. Only lessons to carry forward.

We should try to rest in the middle place between excitement and fear, between joy and sorrow. That balance is where peace lives. And in that stillness, the soul finds room to grow and to thrive.

Index

Contents

Poems

1. LIFE IN CINDERELLA'S SHOES

If there is a piece of the puzzle, it will only fit the puzzle it belongs to—and the puzzle will be completed only when the last piece has made its way to the puzzle.

An old tale of Cinderella is known by one and all. The customized magical shoes could only fit Cinderella and no one else.

Has it ever felt like some positions keep on vacating until they find the right fit?

Life is just the same. It has to fit in the shoes it belongs to, and the shoes have to find a way for the life to complete.

Whether it is about people in life, a goal, a task, a responsibility, or a role—it will only work when it is the right fit.

If it isn't the right fit, the walk will be painful until you get rid of the misfit.

And if you don't get rid of the misfit, the misfit will tire, wear out, and give up eventually.

One way or another, it will separate if it wasn't meant to be.

So, if it ever feels raw—missing a piece of the puzzle—just imagine the magical shoes. It has to fit, or it will never fit.

It's not just about one; it's about one and all—whether it would all fit together.

Find the best fit, and fit in the best find, and life will become a smooth walk in beautiful Cinderella's shoes!

Photograph by: Dr. Jaya Sonkar MD MPH

2. PURSUIT OF CHASE OR PURSUIT OF PEACE?

One day, I stepped out onto the balcony of my beach house, felt the sea breeze on my skin, had the most beautiful girl in town inside my home, and a Porsche in my garage. I thought to myself, this is what I've dreamed of all my life.

But now that it was finally here, it didn't feel any different. It didn't give me the thrill I had imagined. I still felt like the same child—wondering what more I needed to keep myself amused.

I was still the same inside, unchanged, and uncertain about what to do next.

It was as if everything I had chased all this time

wasn't as amazing as I thought it would be, says Mr. Smith.

I've lived an interesting life. Now in my 90s, I come from a hippie culture. I've been there, done it all, and I'm still standing. I have children, lost three wives along the way—two to life, and one through separation. And yet, I still feel like there's something I'm searching for.

Mr. Smith's story, in a way, resembles many others in one common truth:

Sometimes, it's the chase we're chasing—not the goal itself. Our minds crave activity. They thrive in motion. But once we reach the destination, we must learn to cherish the stability while it lasts—because instability will find its way back eventually. When we do arrive at a place of calm, learning to maintain that fragile balance—an unstable equilibrium—with peace, is what fosters true strength.

In our pursuit of a goal, we often miss the journey, too focused on the finish line. But it's within the journey that the real richness lies—the experiences, the lessons, the growth, and the delicate balance of life that we learn to manage.

Because in the end, stability and peace are what we ultimately seek—to truly rest in peace.

If we've done what we set out to do, and reached where we were meant to, we must also learn to remain there—with joy and grace.

Often, we keep setting new goals, and that's not a bad thing. We want to explore the full extent of our abilities.

But when it comes to wants, there's wisdom in identifying a point of comfort and choosing not to endlessly increase those desires. That's where peace and stability are born.

Not craving the next "want" doesn't mean abandoning growth—it means being content where we are, while still using our potential fully. That balance can lead to both success and serenity.

It's the path where we encounter new things— flowers, berries, animals, landscapes, people. And it's the destination that gives us the stillness to reflect on everything the path brought us.

Both the pursuit and the reward matter.

We should remain active and purposeful—but not frantic in our pursuit. Let the next phase come from a peaceful mind, stepping into a new journey with grace. And when we finally reach the summit of the mountain—we must remember to pause, lift our binoculars, and take in the beauty of the path we climbed.

Photograph by: Dr. Jaya Sonkar MD MPH

3. BACK TO SQUARE ONE, BUT WITH A PERSPECTIVE

Q. Does spirituality mean altruism?
A. No.

Q. Does austerity mean denunciation?
A. No.

Q. Does kindness mean it's okay to accept harm?
A. No.

Q. Does letting go mean being insensitive?
A. No.

Q. Does indifference mean ignorance?
A. No.

Q. Is it possible to come back to square one after attaining self-awareness?
A. Yes.

If we stand on a mountain peak with our eyes closed, we are 'there', but 'not really there'.
If we open our eyes, we are there, we are truly present, and we become aware of everything around us.

We can still do everything, live life the same way, do business, pursue education, travel, dance, host parties, but we begin to operate from an enlightened stage. A stage where we are more conscious:

Of what is there,
Of what won't be there,
Of what's temporary,
Of what's meaningful,
Of what's truly important.

It's like knowing the game of life before playing it.
It's like making an informed decision.
It's like opening a third eye.
It's like being in the same place, doing the same things, returning to square one... but with a perspective.

Let's come together to explore the inner world, awaken our senses, and step into Spirituality 101. Let's begin the journey, with meditation.

Meditation Techniques to Get Started

Here are a few simple yet powerful meditation practices that can help cultivate inner awareness and clarity:

Silent Sitting
Sit quietly in a comfortable position with your eyes closed. Allow your thoughts to pass without resistance. Observe them like a spectator, without judgment or analysis. This helps train your mind to detach and witness rather than react.

Focused Reflection
It's okay to think deeply about something that truly matters to you. Gently hold that thought and explore it from all angles. This is not overthinking, this is mindful contemplation.

Breath Awareness
Focus on your breathing. Feel the air move in and out of your nostrils or notice the rise and fall of your chest. Let your breath anchor you to the present moment.

Chanting or Mantra Repetition

Repeat a word, phrase, or sound, silently or aloud. This could be a spiritual mantra or simply a calming sound like "Om." The rhythm helps center the mind.

Trataka (Candle Gazing)

In a dark room, stare at the blue part of a candle flame for a few seconds. Then close your eyes and observe the image of the flame within. This enhances concentration and visual focus.

Target Staring

Choose a fixed point or object and focus on it steadily for a few minutes without blinking. This trains the mind to stay anchored and undistracted.

Singing or Note Practice

Using your voice as a tool, either by singing, humming, or doing basic note practice, can be incredibly meditative. Sound vibrations affect the mind and body deeply.

Puzzle Solving

Even solving puzzles can be a form of meditation. When done mindfully, it sharpens focus and brings mental clarity while keeping the mind engaged in a positive challenge.

These practices help you build the ability to focus on what truly matters, while reducing the noise, both external and internal. Over time, they allow you to become more aware of your surroundings, your emotions, and your inner world.

Let's step into a deeper inside
Which opens into a wider outside.

Photograph by: Dr. Jaya Sonkar MD MPH

4. LIKABILITY

Do people like you?
Maybe.
Maybe not.

Do you like anyone?
Maybe.
Maybe not.

Everyone is the lead character in their own lives. No one plays a supporting or second role in their own story.

Everyone is the center of their lives and wants to see things around them in their favor. And there is nothing wrong with it.

That means that everyone likes themselves, and whatever else they like or whoever else they like matches up with something around their lives.

Likability is self-centric.
Anyone likes anyone because some form of need is being fulfilled.

It can be a very kind need or an unkind one. But some need, some wish, or some purpose is being met, giving rise to likability.

- No one likes being beat up.
- No one likes being mistreated.
- No one likes to be ignored.
- No one likes to feel small about themselves.
- No one likes to feel dejected.

On the other hand:
- Everyone likes to feel valued.
- Everyone likes to feel loved.
- Everyone likes to be respected.
- Everyone likes to be cared for.
- Everyone likes to be heard.
- Everyone likes to be centered.
- Everyone likes to feel good about themselves.
- Everyone likes to be nurtured.
- Everyone likes a comfort zone.

Something or the other is always being met before the spark of likability ignites.

And all of it has to be absent, and negative stimulus present, before likability ends, dislike begins, or indifference sets in.

So when we like someone, it's truly what we like about ourselves in the presence of that likable someone.

No one starts liking someone who has caused them harm. Everyone starts liking someone when that person brings positive influence.

So: I like him. I like her. She likes me. He likes me. Or even: We love someone, or someone loves us. These are all subjective.

Some pull or push is always working when someone likes or dislikes someone.

People who were once close drift apart when the symbiosis ends or the commensalism stops.

A Personal Example

A few days ago, I went to a restaurant. While enjoying my meal, I met an old man who didn't know anything about Indian food.

He asked me if I knew what those black ball-like things were and if they were good.

I told him excitedly that those are called gulab jamun. Then he had some more questions.

I took my time to explain each dish in the buffet, the best way to eat it and which items should be packed separately. By the time we were done setting our plates, we were both very pleased to have met.

I felt happy helping the old man relish Indian food for the first time, and he was happy to get authentic recommendations.

A very pleasant experience, indeed, a likable one.

In My Work

Similarly, when I meet patients, all of them are close to my heart. They make me feel fulfilled by allowing me to help them.

However, some patients leave a deep impact through their kind gestures and their trust in care. That trust motivates me to go above and beyond, whether it is possible or not.

While the care remains the same for everyone, such people certainly spark the magic of likability.

The Essence of Likability

That being said, we don't need to bend ourselves backwards, nor do we need to leave ourselves behind to become someone else to experience likability.

Because people don't really like you. They like themselves, and how you make them feel.

Stay yourself. Stay kind. Stay positive. Create a genuine aura around you, and the people with the same frequency will resonate. They will enter your circle of likability, because they like themselves, and your presence helps them like themselves even more.

So, be likable or not, just make sure to be yourself, and be kind.

What makes the Mona Lisa so universally likable?

5. MY PERFECT MOON!

Is the Grass Greener on the Other Side? Or Do We Have It Greener on Ours?

I got my new telescope.
I looked at the moon.

My pretty moon,
That was a perfect circle.

Wasn't perfect anymore.
Its edges were uneven.
It had pits and holes.

It was still the same moon.
It hadn't changed.
Only I could see it better.
It was the same as before,
Just that my view was enhanced.

It is said:
Door ke dhol suhavane.

English Translation:
The things that are farther are more attractive.

A similar idiom is:
The grass is greener on the other side.

While we live on Mother Earth.
And Mother Earth gives us life.
We have the luxury to enjoy.
The beauty of our moon, other planets, and even the sun, which we know are not habitable.

The extreme temperatures there cannot sustain life.
The things that are farther look perfect.
It is only when we see through a microscope that we can observe every cell and know it better.

But once we know it, it is sometimes a good idea to step back and enjoy its beauty without analyzing it in detail.
Because the more perfect things appear, the more content we feel.
And that contentment helps us overlook the finer imperfections of those who are near us.

When we are done exploring the finer details.
It becomes more enjoyable to embrace the imperfections.
And appreciate the perfect distant picture.

Let us enjoy the beauty of our moons!

Photograph by: Dr. Jaya Sonkar MD MPH

Poems

Dr. Jaya Sonkar MD MPH

1. IMPERMANENCE

Everything has a timeline
Everything has a lifeline
Everything has a beginning
Everything has an end

Nothing is here to stay
Nothing is there to last
While things seem to move slow
Within a blink, they go too fast

It's the sand that will slip
It's beyond anyone's grip
It's the wind that will blow
It's the water that will flow

It's the wave that will soar
It's the rain that will pour
It's the thunder that will roar
It will see its own door

Know yourself
Prioritize yourself
Love yourself
Cherish yourself

Nothing and no one will
Last forever
The only one to stay till the end
Is you yourself, my dear friend

Know your element and become it
Accomplish your goals
Fulfill your desire
Stay harmless to others,
And also yourself!

Photograph by: Dr. Jaya Sonkar MD MPH

2. WHO OWES WHOM?

The rain owes the clouds
The clouds owe the sea
The sea owes the rivers
The river owes the rain

The carnivores owe the herbivores
The herbivores owe the grass
The grass owes the soil
The soil owes all animals

The wisdom owes its root to the pain
The pain owes its spark to fun
The fun owes its ease to health and wealth
And health and wealth owe the wisdom

The diamond owes the admirers
The admirers owe the diamond

The lotus owes the mud
The mud owes the lotus

The chicken owes the egg
The egg owes the chicken

The taker owes the giver
The giver owes the taker

The taker can be the giver
The giver can be the taker

What goes around
Comes around
What rises, falls
What falls, rises

Life is a wave
It rises
It falls
It rises again

And so on
So who owes whom?

No one owes no one
And everyone owes everyone

Live the life
Full of gratitude
And
Free of Debt

Fly, Rise, Elevate, Lighten,
Bind, but freely and wilfully
Leave, but with care and love
Live with grace,
Freely, yet thankfully!

Photograph by: Dr. Jaya Sonkar MD MPH

3. THE BEAUTIFUL NIGHT!

It's dark
It helps see colors with closed eyes

It's dark
It helps to see the moon shine bright

It's dark
It sharpens and steadies the mind

It's dark
It helps the emotions unwind

It's dark
It opens the mind's eyes and enhances sight

It's dark
It's helps to relish and cherish the sunlight
It is indeed a beautiful night!

Photograph by: Dr. Jaya Sonkar MD MPH

4. RAYS OF LIGHT WHATEVER HAPPENS, HAPPENS FOR GOOD!

Thanks to everyone who said yes to me
Because of them, I am firmly rooted

Thanks to everyone who said No to me
Because of them, I could discover my hidden
capabilities

Thanks to every success that rewarded my hard
work
Because of that, I was able to make a positive
change

Thanks to every failure that made me work harder
Because of that, I mastered the skill and stayed
grounded

Thanks to every friend who held my hand
Because of them, I experienced the warmth and
support

Thanks to every foe
Because of them, I learned to stay alert and wise

Thanks to every estranged friend
Because of them, I became more self reliant and
detached.

Thanks to everyone who cheated
Because of them, I learned to use trust wisely

Thanks to all the experiences, positive or negative
Because of those, I learned to pick up the gems on
the way and not collect just the stones.

Thanks to the life
Because it added to my bag of wisdom

Thanks to the death
Because it helped me value the life

The idiom
'Jo Bhi Hota Hai, Achiever Ke Liye Hota Hai'
(English Translation: 'Whatever happens, happens for good')
was probably created by a very learned soul.

It takes a lifetime of experiences to truly understand this one line!

Photograph by: Dr. Jaya Sonkar MD MPH

5. A VERY LONG DAY

Prologue

It's said, "Ek aur Ek Gyarah." in Hindi.

In English, it means, when one and one come together, their strength feels like eleven, not just two.

And when you find your other one, that's how comforting and beautiful the day can feel.

A Very Long Day!

It's been a very long day
It's been a very tough day
You had one, and I had one
Now you are just sitting
At the end of the day

I come to you,
In your lap I lay,
And say

Would you brush your fingers through my hair?
Would you, one more time, show me the same
care?
Would you see me through all my layers?
Would you rescue me from despair?

You say yes
And pull me to you
You say yes
And hide me in you
You say yes
And brush your fingers through my hair
You say yes
And look at me with care

We've been through the storms
We've been through the floods
We've been through the winds
We've been through the mud

We've held hands
And never let go
We've seen a werewolf
In each other
And chose to stay
Even if it kills

We've held hands
And never let go
We've seen a god
In each other
And chose to stay
And get healed

We've held our heads high
With pride in knowing each other
We've been through thick and thin
Together we cherish, together we suffer

We've had long days
We've had tough days

And at the end of the day
It all melts away

When I come lay in your lap
And you brush your fingers through my hair
And hug me like a big bear
And rescue us from despair

And love, love, love, forever…

Dr. Jaya Sonkar MD MPH

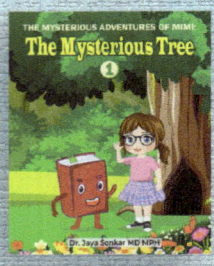

THE MYSTERIOUS ADVENTURES OF MIMI:
The Mysterious Tree
①
Dr. Jaya Sonkar MD MPH

THE MYSTERIOUS ADVENTURES OF MIMI:
THE MYSTERIOUS GLASSES
②
Dr. Jaya Sonkar MD MPH

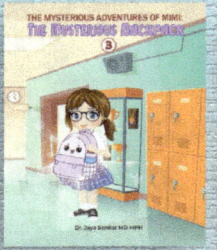

THE MYSTERIOUS ADVENTURES OF MIMI:
THE MYSTERIOUS BACKPACK
③
Dr. Jaya Sonkar MD MPH

THE MYSTERIOUS ADVENTURES OF MIMI:
THE MAGICAL MIRROR
④
Dr. Jaya Sonkar MD MPH

THE MYSTERIOUS ADVENTURES OF MIMI:
MIMI AND THE MYSTERY OF THE SPARKLY DUST
⑤
Dr. Jaya Sonkar MD MPH

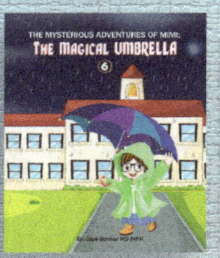

THE MYSTERIOUS ADVENTURES OF MIMI:
THE MAGICAL UMBRELLA
⑥
Dr. Jaya Sonkar MD MPH

THE MYSTERIOUS ADVENTURES OF MIMI:
THE MAGIC TRASH CAN
⑦
Dr. Jaya Sonkar MD MPH

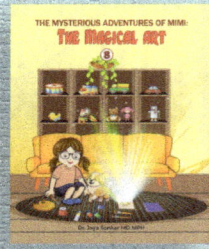

THE MYSTERIOUS ADVENTURES OF MIMI:
THE MAGICAL ART
⑧
Dr. Jaya Sonkar MD MPH

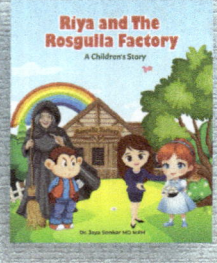

Riya and The Rosgulla Factory
A Children's Story
Dr. Jaya Sonkar MD MPH

Ridiculously Simplified Rheumatology
The Story Of Me. Gout!
VOL 1
Dr. Jaya Sonkar
MD, MPH

THE MYSTERIOUS ADVENTURES OF MIMI:
MIMI AND THE COPYCAT
⑨
Dr. Jaya Sonkar MD MPH

JEEVAN GYAN
Life Lessons
Dr. Jaya Sonkar MD MPH

Insights
Dr. Jaya Sonkar MD MPH

INSIGHTS 2
REFLECTION AND INTROSPECTION
DR. JAYA SONKAR, MD MPH

Insights 3
A Journey Beyond Boundaries
Dr. Jaya Sonkar, MD MPH

Insights 4
The Path
Dr. Jaya Sonkar, MD MPH

THE END